ACKNOWLEDGEMENTS
Editor: A Goss

PHOTOGRAPHY, ART & FONTS:
Images, photography and artwork credited to alonasavchuk, tetiana-pavliuchenko, Slowmotiongli,
Wrangel, Andres Alvarado, George Peters, Nikola Art, Tony Beck, StudioG, stu-khaii, dkdesignz,
spanhoven, Geoview, Parkol, Kung Mangkorn, Mark Kostich, Kengoru, Ken Canning, SDominick, ohgd-
uk, vintage-illustrations, Suzine's Images, Getty Images, Pixabay and Canva Creative Studio all
obtained for commercial use via Canva Pro Content License.

Goss
CASTLE

This book belongs to

···

Contents

An animal so furry, moving slow,

Hanging from a tree, by just its toes.

A cute round face, and a great big smile,

Let's learn about sloths for a while...

There are two species of sloths in the world.

Two-toed sloths and three-toed sloths.

Here is a two-toed sloth, called a **Choloepus** sloth.

It has **two claws** on its front limbs and three claws on its back limbs.

Two-toed sloths are a little bit bigger than three-toed sloths.

Here is a three-toed sloth, called a **Bradypus** sloth.

It has **three claws** on all four of its limbs.

Having just three claws doesn't stop a sloth from being an excellent tree-climber.

Imagine if you had just three fingers!

How would you describe what a sloth looks like?

Do you think they look happy or sad?

What do you think this sloth is thinking about?

Sloths might look a bit like **monkeys**,

but they're actually related to **armadillos**

and **anteaters**.

Sloths live in the **rainforests** of Central America and South America, in countries like Brazil, Peru and Ecuador.

Sloths have been around since dinosaurs ruled the world sixty-five million years ago.

You might think sloths need to be able to see really well, but actually a sloth's **eyesight** is very poor.

Sloths can't see at all in bright daylight because their eyes don't have any cone cells.

They take their time to move slowly, making sure they don't bump into anything or fall out of trees.

A sloth's eyes might not be great at seeing, but its **nose** is very good at smelling!

Sloths use their nostrils to sniff out juicy fruits to eat.

A sloth's sense of smell is very strong.

Can you smell fruit from far away?

Sloths love to munch on leaves and fruits that they find in the rainforest.

They don't need to eat very much, because they don't move very much.

It takes sloths a long time to digest food – up to thirty days just to digest a leaf.

Do you eat slowly or quickly?

When they're not having a bite to eat, sloths are very happy to slowly hang around in the tops of trees.

Baby sloths are born with fully formed claws, which help them hang from trees all day long.

Female sloths give birth once a year, and a baby sloth will stay with its mother for six months.

Whilst sloths spend almost all of their time up high in trees, about once a week they slowly climb all the way down to the forest floor. They dig a little hole to poop into.

Even sloths need to poop!

Sloths look cute and cuddly, but they can also be quite dirty. Because sloths move so slowly, their fur can be covered in **green algae**.

A sloth's fur is home to fungi and lots of insects, like sloth-moths.

Insects are happy to have a nice warm home, and sloths are happy to be covered in green, which means they can't be seen by hungry hawks and jaguars in the trees.

Can you stay as still as a sloth?

A sloth lives most of its life in the tall rainforest trees.

Sloths even **sleep** way up high – often upside down!

They also use their long curved claws to grab onto a branch or two, curl up, and sleep for up to **twenty hours** a day.

How long do you sleep for?

EVEN MORE
FACTS ABOUT SLOTHS

The word '**sloth**' means '**slow**' or '**lazy**'.

One of the biggest dangers for sloths is their home getting destroyed. Humans cutting down trees is called **deforestation**.

Long ago, before you were born, there used to be **giant sloths**. These giant sloths lived on the ground and could be over **six metres** tall!

Sloths are super swimmers. They can swim up to three times faster than they can walk. Sloths might be very slow in trees and on land, but if you see a sloth in a river, just watch it go!

Sloths can live between twenty to fifty years but no one really knows exactly how long they usually live for in the wild.

There's so much more we can learn about sloths.

SLOTH QUIZ

Question 1.   True or False? Baby sloths are born with their claws already made.

Question 2.   How long do sloths usually sleep for each day?

Question 3.   What does the word 'sloth' mean?

Question 4.   True or False? Sloths have very good eyesight.

Question 5.   Which two animals are sloths closely related to?

Answer 1. True. Baby sloths are born with their claws already made. Answer 2. Sloths usually sleep for up to 20 hours each day. Answer 3. The word 'sloth' means 'slow' or 'lazy'. Answer 4. False. Sloths have poor eyesight. Answer 5. Armadillos and Ant-eaters are closely related to sloths.

DRAW YOUR OWN SLOTH

If you enjoyed the book, please leave a review on Amazon.

Your reviews help us get more kids learning through reading!

1. Visit **Amazon**
2. Click **Orders**
3. Find the book and click **Write a Product Review**

Thank you

Goss
CASTLE

Complete your Goss Castle bookshelf today

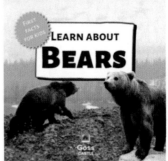

Get your freebies and excellent learning resources by subscribing to the Goss Castle newsletter at **gosscastle.com**